All About Aries

C
to
fo

ALL ABOUT

ARIES

A Charming Zodiac Profile

By Dean Walley

Illustrated by Lois Jackson

HALLMARK EDITIONS

Here's a book you can carry
Wherever you go…
It tells you the things
Every Aries should know!

When you lose your temper,
everyone had better look out!

You're probably fond
of potatoes and meat.
You'll need to be careful
that's not all that you eat.

You're a good pioneer.

Regardless of the weather,
you have a way
of staying sunny…

Doing something more than twice

can put your patience

to the test.

But it's easy for you
to overdo it.
Take life as it comes, Aries!

Love and work
are the two things
that set you apart…

Aries:

The Sign of the Ram

Ruler: *Mars*

Color: *Red*

Gem: *Diamond*

Harmonious Signs:

Sagittarius, Leo